The Soul
and A Loaf of Bread

The Soul
and A Loaf of Bread

The Teachings of Sheikh Abol-Hasan of Kharaqan

Renditions by Vraje Abramian

HOHM PRESS
Prescott, Arizona

Interior Design and Layout: Zachary Parker, www.kadakgraphics.com

Library of Congress Cataloging-in-Publication Data

_K_harqani, _K_hvajah Abulhasan, 967-1033.
[Nur al-'ulum. English]
The soul and a loaf of bread : the teachings of Sheikh Abol-Hasan of Kharaqan / renditions by Vraje Abramian.
    p. cm.
ISBN 978-1-935387-12-1 (trade pbk. : alk. paper)
1. Sufism--Early works to 1800. I. Abramian, Vraje. II. Title.
BP188.9.K4313 2010
297.4'4--dc22
                            2010000622

HOHM PRESS
P.O. Box 2501
Prescott, AZ 86302
800-381-2700
http://www.hohmpress.com

This book was printed in the U.S.A. on recycled, acid-free paper using soy ink.

Cover design by Massoud Mansouri is from a 13th-century Iranian decorative plate. The young man—having abandoned his ego, symbolized by the horse, and left behind the five vices which plague it (lust, anger, greed, vanity and attachment)—is contemplating his soul, symbolized by the female figure asleep in the ocean of Eternity. The Arabic script is in exaltation of water and the fact that all life emanates from it.

Sheikh Abol-Hasan's Tomb, Kharaqan, Iran

Whoever knocks on this door, feed him and ask not of his faith, for if he deserved a soul from his Creator, he certainly deserves a loaf of bread from Abol-Hasan.

—Sheikh Abol-Hasan Kharaqani

*Humbly dedicated to Huzur
and his successor, Baba Ji.*

*The Lover faces God in Adoration,
and the disciple adores his face;
the Lover becomes a Messenger,
for the disciple to behold The Message;
the Lover is God's charge,
the disciple, the Lover's.*
—Sheikh Abol-Hasan

ACKNOWLEDGEMENTS

Sincere thanks are due to Mr. Massoud Mansouri for his refinement, generosity and humility; and for his artwork, which adorns the cover of this book, as well as the covers of *Nobody, Son of Nobody* (Hohm Press, 2001) and *This Heavenly Wine* (Hohm Press, 2006); to my wife Elizabeth Ruth for her infinite patience with me, and to Regina S. Ryan, editor, Hohm Press.

CONTENTS

PREFACE

The Tao that can be described is not the Tao.
The name that can be named is not the eternal name.
The nameless is the beginning of heaven and earth.

—Lao Tsu

It is said that this material plane of existence, where life survives on life, and at birth one joins a long queue at death's gate, can become a most effective learning place if one has the good fortune of crossing paths with a fully realized soul, a perfect saint or mystic. By dying to themselves, annihilating their ego, perfect mystics return to and merge in that ever present consciousness always eclipsed by one's ego. They thus become living proofs of that understanding which makes this journey in the shadow of death, meaningful and bearable.

The perfect mystics teach that consciousness—infinite, endless and beginningless—is that Presence which fills silence. When approached with words, this Presence turns into a mystery, they say, and is given different names in different places and times, for example, Allah, Olodumare, God, Sat Purush, the Great Void, the Tao, and others. We are told that this Presence wills forth existence, the initial manifestations of which are in the form of sound[1] and light detectable to inner human faculties. These faculties are activated when our head is emptied of that ever present storm that blows through it in the form of thoughts, hopes, fears, desires, and other mental forms of activity. Any discipline aimed at bringing about full realization

---

1 In different traditions this sound is known as *Shabd,* Logos, the Word, *Nedaye Asmani,* the Music of the Spheres.

of human potential, they say, essentially struggles to release human perception from the grip of that faculty which manufactures, and then occupies itself with, this storm—namely, the human mind.

If life beyond mind sounds like an impossibility, it is because we are convinced that we are *nothing but* mind and body. In truth, the mystics say, we are that particle of the Infinite Consciousness which, while vitalizing our mind, is shrouded by it. They say that if the fog of mind (ego) lifts but for a split second, one experiences the Presence directly and remembers that peace which "surpasseth all understanding."

Those who go through this experience of realizing the Presence may become troubadours of the Divine and sing of the unspeakable glory they witness. Or, they may choose lives of quiet contemplation and service—Sheikh Abol-Hasan Kharaqani (died 1034) was one such character. He was born in the village of Kharaqan in Khorasan[2] and never left there. He was an unlettered man[3], a farmer and a gardener, who toiled all his life and personally maintained his Khaneqah'[4], which was open to all regardless of cast or creed. He was a spiritual emperor to whose generous table many spiritual and temporal rulers came for alms.

Among those who came to Sheikh Abol-Hasan for spiritual uplift were such Sufi[5] luminaries as Shiekh Abu-Saeed Abil-

---

2 Khorasan: Today the northeastern province of Khorasan in Iran borders Afghanistan and northern Pakistan. In the 10th century, it denoted a vast region which included western Afghanistan and the regions north of the Oxus River (Transoxania) which were later to become Tajikistan, Uzbekistan, Turkmenistan, etc. Khorasan has boasted an ancient tradition of God-intoxicated individuals who taught long before Islam arrived in the region, and whose teachings deeply influenced mystic Islam, i.e., Sufism.

3 It is said that Sheikh Abol-Hasan was graced with the ability to read the Qoraan while keeping a nightly vigil at the tomb of Abu-Yazid Bastami (Bayazid, died 875), to whom he was particularly devoted.

4 A Sufi lodge where the poor and the wayfarer are welcome.

5 Sufis are Muslim mystics.

Kheir and Khaje Abdollah Ansari of Herat. Rulers and warlords came as well, and humbled by the Sheikh's humility, left much changed. To this day Kharaqani is held in highest esteem and venerated above most by those in the region whose main purpose in life is to hone and refine their perceptions toward fully realizing their human potential.

In this collection, Sheikh Kharaqani's statements, collected and recorded by his companions, have been rendered into English for the international reader in the belief that contemplation of the mystics' sayings, be it a thousand years later and in an "alien" language, is one way to cross paths with them, for time and place have no hold where they are. What is dearest to them is a heart longing in earnest for that heritage we humans, enmeshed in the grossness of material existence, are apt to forget.

I was given a wish by my Lord and I said,
"Beloved, I want all those who were in existence when I was,
those who after my passing will come to visit my grave,
those who won't, those who heard my name,
and those who never did, to be forgiven and to go free."
In my heart I heard, "In life you did what I wanted,
* now I will do that which you wish."*
—Sheikh Abol-Hasan Kharaqani

A SHORT BIOGRAPHY

Our Sheikh Said,
My body is to work and replenish the earth,
my tongue, to speak of this Love,
and my head to lay at my Beloved's feet
in surrender.

Within that ocean of light which has been called the Persianate Sufism, there is an ancient lighthouse who still aids wayfarers seeking to reach home. This humble emperor is known as Sheikh Abol-Hasan of Kharaqan (d. 1034). He was a farmer and a gardener by profession, an unlettered villager who toiled his entire life and never left Kharaqan, a small village near Bastam in present day Shahrood area, in north-central Iran.[1] It is generally thought that Sheikh Abol-Hasan was guided by Abol-Abbas Qassab Amolee, whose disciples included such luminaries as Sheikh Abu-Saeed Ibn Abil-Kheir.[2]

Sheikh Abol-Hasan considered Abu-Yazid Bastami (Bayazid, d. 875)—a great Sufi saint who lived in Bastam two hundred years before him—his greatest spiritual confidant, the one who "taught" him how to recite the Quraan. He never claimed any disciples and always warned seekers to shun worldly fame and glamour. His Khaniqah, or Sufi lodge, is said to have been the only one in tenth century Iran that was founded and solely supported by personal income.

---

1 This area used to be considered part of Khorasan, an ancient eastern province which included western Afghanistan as well as major parts of Trans-Oxanian Central Asia, present day Tajikistan, Turkmenistan and Uzbekistan.
2 See *Nobody Son of Nobody*, Vraje Abramian, translator. Prescott, Arizona: Hohm Press, 2001.

The entrance to the Sheikh's tomb in Kharaqan.

Sheikh Abol-Hasan professed allegiance to no particular Sufi order; though many orders mention him in their genealogy. The Naqshbandis in particular consider him as one of their own through Abu-Ali Farmazi (d. 1084).

Kharaqani's main premise is that human desire for God is an affair that begins not with the individual but with God, who planted the seed on the day before the first day, and who summons and gradually brings the individual closer and closer until Reunion.[3]

---

3 Kadkani, Dr. Mohammad Reza Shafiee. *Neveshte-bar-darya, az miras-e erfani-e Sheikh Abol-Hasan-e Kharaqani* (Original Farsi): *Scripture on the Sea, from Spiritual Legacy of Sheikh Abol-Hasan of Kharaqan.* Tehran, Iran: Sokhan Publications,1988, pp. 23-135. (NbD)

The view of the tomb from the north.

This idea is by no means unique in the Sufi view of human existence:

Abol-Abbas Qassab Amolee (tenth century, Khorasan), Sheikh Abol-Hasan's reputed guide, is quoted saying, "... if you were to be asked if you know God, do not say yes, for this would be an arrogant conjecture; and do not say no, for that would be a disgraceful denial, say instead, may He himself make himself known to us, for this is not within our reach."[4]

Ibn-Ataollah, the thirteenth century Egyptian, Shadhili Sufi saint says, "If you were to be united with God only after your arrogant vices were effaced, you would never be united with

4 Kadkani, NbD, pp 65-66.

A meditation cave near the western wall of the tomb.

him. But when He wants to unite you with himself, your qualities and attributes are covered in his and by virtue of what comes from him to you, not by what goes from you to him, this Union happens."[5]

And **Attar** says, "... it all comes not from intellect, but from Him (God) and in Him, it ends."[6]

Commentaries From Others

Not much exists about Kharaqani's personal life, other than the fact that he lived at a time of great, ongoing turmoil and warfare in a region replete with small kingdoms and Khanates. To have a glimpse at the Sheikh's character, it would perhaps be best to look at him through the eyes of some of the greatest Sufi luminaries who have commented on him.[7]

Sheikh-ol-Eshraq-Suhravardi Maqtul[8] (d. 1191), a Sufi mystic/theologian who was killed in Allepo, Syria for his uncompromising views, refers to Qhassab Amolee, Mansour Hallaj, Abu-Yazid Bastami (Bayazid) and Shiekh Abol-Hasan Kharaqani as the four foundational characters who continued the "Tariq-e Khosravan," the ancient Iranian School of Royal Wisdom[9].

---

5 Danner, V., Thackson, W.M., and Annemarie Shimmel. "Ibn Ata' Illah. The Book of Wisdom, Kwaja Abdullah Ansari, Intimate Conversations." In: *The Classics of Western Spirituality*. New York: Paulist Press, 1978, p.79.

6 NbD, p.65.

7 NbD, pp. 385-481.

8 For more on Suhravadi see: S.H. Nasr, "The Spread of Illuminationist School of Suhravadi," *Islamic Quarterly*, 14. *Also see*: "The School of Isfahan" in *A History of Muslim Philosophy*, edited by H.M. Sharif, 1966.

9 What is referred to as "Tariq-e Khosravan," the Royal Wisdom (or Path), is very difficult to trace in history, for all pre-Islamic religious and spiritual traditions had to go underground after the Arab conquest of the Persian Empire in the seventh century. Popular history attaches occult powers to the "Moqhs" (Latinized as the "Maji"), the Zoroastrian priests. The famous Christian nativity characters, the "three Kings from the East," are generally agreed to be three Maji from Iran who had followed the star under which Jesus

Attar (d. 1230?)—of whom Rumi said, "He has traversed the seven cities of Love and I am at the corner of the first alley."—in his "Tazkarat-ol Olya" (the History of the Saints), says, "... the Pole of his time Abol-Hasan of Kharaqan ... was the King of the Path ... owner of the secrets of the Truth and ... in boldness (*gostakhee*[10], Persian) on the path of Love of such caliber that could not be described."[11]

Abu-Yazid of Bastam (Bayazid) (d. 855), another giant Khorasanian mystic, is said to have visited a certain Dehestan village regularly, and while passing through Kharaqan on his

---

of Nazareth was to take birth, and to bring him their good will. What is historically evident, however, is that initiatory spiritual practices of Persian origin, such as the Mazdaki and Manichean disciplines, which, judging from the sheer ferocity of the reactions they caused in the religious establishments in Zoroastrian, and later Christian, dominions, had to have been effective methods in awakening large numbers of people. And they did not continue. Or did they? Since in no socio/political upheaval do the spiritual practices of nations shift overnight, it is reasonable to assume that the Persian spiritual traditions adapted to the new parameters and performed their due share in nurturing that brand of Islamic mysticism referred to as the School of Ecstatic Love, or the Khorasanian School of Sufism. Khorasan, the eastern-most frontier land of Islam, was at a geopolitically safe distance from Baghdad, the seat of the Khaliphate, and thus provided a relatively safe haven for those differing from the Khalifate. For more on this, *see*: H. Corbin, *Societe Iranologie*, Vol. 3, 1946.

10 *Gostakh* (Persian): bold, arrogant, one with a disregard for accepted ways and dogma; unafraid, brave.In Sufi lore it often denotes one at such a high spiritual station as to be beyond the reach of standard human norms of conduct, an attribute of one in ecstasy. The example of Mansour Hallaj, and his utterance, "Ana-ol-Haqq." (I am the Truth), is perhaps the most famous example of such boldness. But there are others: Bayazid's famous statement, "Praise be to me, how great is my Glory," was no less shocking to the uninitiated. And in "Maqalat-e Shams Tabriz: the Essays of Shams Tabriz," (J.M. Sadeghi, p 252), we read, "I am not one to run after anyone... if one avoids me, I avoid him ten times worse. God greets me ten times, I do not reply. After the tenth time, I half-acknowledge and then play deaf."! And Kharaqani said, "The Sufi is not a created being." This statement created an uproar and originated many commentaries and arguments.

These are bewildering statements by those whose station, as lovers annihilated in the Beloved, gives them the "boldness" to speak with the Beloved's tongue. Perhaps the best way to treat them would be to follow the advice of Najm Razi (d.1221) who says, "Lovers' words are to be shielded in secrecy and not made public."

11 translated by V. Abramian, from "Tazkarat-ol-Olya," *Biography of the Saints* by Attar Neishaboori (original Farsi). Edited Dr. M. Estelaamee, Zavvar Publications, 1994.

way, to have always stopped and breathed in deeply. When his bewildered disciples inquired, Bayazid said,

"There will be a man in this village three times my senior in that he will till the land, plant trees, and raise a family."[12]

Shams of Tabriz (died 1248), the one who caused Molana Jalaleddin Balkhi, known as Rumi, to leave theological/academic heresay and experience that Presence where words cease, was a stern teacher who, in his own words, "... was not interested in training disciples, but Masters, and then the highest[13], the perfect ones!" He says in his *Maqalat*, "Sheikh Abol-Hasan was a great man ...", and then he proceeds to tell the famous story of Sultan Mahmood Qhaznavi, who traveled a great distance to Kharaqan to see the saint. Pitching his tent near Sheikh Abol-Hasan's Sufi lodge, the Sultan sent a message requesting him to come to his tent and see him. When the saint refused, Sultan Qhaznavi sent another emissary who had been instructed to recite this verse from the Quraan: "You who believe, obey God, his Messenger, and those of you in authority." Upon hearing this, Sheikh Abol-Hasan tells the emissary,

"Tell Sultan Mahmood that I am so lost in obeying God that I have not yet gotten to the Messenger, let alone those in authority."

The Sultan eventually visited the saint and learned about humility and spiritual poverty, after which the saint sent him away with blessings.

---

12 Ibid., p.661.
13 Maqhalate Shams Tabrizi, pp 44-48 (*Essays by Shams Tabriz*, Jaafar Modarres Sadeqi, Markaz Publications, Tehran, 1995.)

Khaje Abdollah Ansari (d. 1089), the great Pir[14] of Herat said of Sheikh Abol-Hasan, "He (Sheikh Abol-Hasan) is my 'Pir.' I couldn't understand and wondered when I heard that he had said the Sufi is not a created being, so I went to see him. Before I could ask, Sheikh Abol-Hasan said,

> *"O' you who have crossed the sea*
> *and whose beloved I am,*
> *that which eats and drinks is not the Sufi,*
> *that is created, but the*
> *Inner Meaning, where Sufi's true being rests,*
> *That is not created."*

Khaje Abdollah says, "If I had not heard this, I would have kept on confusing ego and body for the Truth."[15] He then says,

> *"I, Abdollah, was a wanderer seeking the*
> *Water of Life, I chanced upon Kharaqani and*
> *drank so much of this Water that neither Abdollah*
> *remained nor Kharaqani; if you have It,*
> *you know what is being said here"[16].*

Khaje Abdollah finally intimates that the word "sea" used by the saint in his greeting, was an answer to a question regarding an inner state which had been causing him bewilderment for a long time; one he had never verbalized but had put to the Sheikh through inner communion.

---

14 Pir : Spiritual guide, Master.
15 NbD, Khaje Abdollah Ansari's statements, pp 387-391. Also see: *Classics of Western Spirituality*, Ibn-Ata'illah and Kwaja Abdullah Ansari, translated by V. Danner and W.M. Thackston, Preface by Annemarie Schimmel, Paulist Press, N.Y., 1978, pp. 168-176.
16 An entire 42-page essay analyzing this theopathic statement by Kharaqani, authored by Najme Razi, is given in NbD, pp. 439-481.

Sheikh Abu-Saeed Ibn-e-Abil-Kheir (d. 1049), the poet and orator that he was, chose silence when he arrived at Sheikh Abol Hasan's abode. Master asked Abu-Saeed to speak:

"You are said to be able to speak beautifully,
speak to us of God's Beauty".

Abu-Saeed replied,

"My words are worthy of those who are seekers;
they are not worthy of an Intimate."

Master said,

"This is not meant to benefit me,
but you will benefit from being heard,"

After which Abu-Saeed began a sermon. Later Abu-Saeed was told by the Master,

"I had begged the Almighty to send me one of his own,
so I could share some of his Secrets with his Friend,
and you are my desire fulfilled."

Before Sheikh Abu-Saeed left, Master said,

"Your road to the Beloved is one of joy and bliss,
mine is one of Longing. Now then, you live in delight
and leave me this Pain, for we are both doing
the Beloved's work."[17]

---

17 NbD, pp.400-412.

THE SOUL AND A LOAF OF BREAD

Sheikh Abdorrahman Jami (d. 1492), the great Naqshbandi master from Khorasan,[18] says of Kharaqani, "... he said,

> *"For forty years my mind has been entertaining the
> thought of a glass of cold, sweet sherbet, or of sour
> yogurt drink and I have yet to oblige."*[19]

Majddeddin Bagdadi (d. 1219) writes that a group of merchants, about to begin a business venture into distant lands, came to the Sheikh and asked for blessings and a prayer to protect them from bandits. He told them to begin their journey in God's name and, should evil come their way, they were to mention Abol-Hasan of Kharaqan. Some frowned at this and said some verses in the Quraan would be more appropriate than mentioning a creature's name; others took the Sheikh's words to heart and left quietly.

Their caravan was indeed accosted by bandits and everyone, except those who mentioned the Sheikh's name, were robbed pitilessly. Upon their return, the merchants went to the saint and exclaimed, "... for God's sake, tell us what this means! Isn't God's name greater than all in his Creation?" "It is so indeed," the Sheikh replied. "Then how do we explain what happened to us?," they asked. Sheikh Abol-Hasan said,

> *"You mentioned a name without realizing the Named,
> whereas those who were spared, mentioned the name
> of the one whom they knew and who is an Intimate
> and a Lover, and this is the same as calling upon Him."*

---

18 For more on Jami, see: *This Heavenly Wine*, Hohm Press, 2005, translated by Vraje Abramian.
19 NbD, p.433, no. 1335.

Majdeddin then adds:

*"This is a truth no one believes except those who have
tasted the Truth and have observed this Affair closely."*[20]

It is said that a disciple once came to Sheikh Abol-Hasan
and asked for his blessing to go and see the spiritual Pole of the
age, who was said to occasionally appear on Mt. Lebanon. The
disciple narrates this story:

> Upon reaching there, I saw a group waiting to pray for
> a deceased whose shrouded corpse was lying in front
> of them. We waited for a long while and I was told we
> were waiting for the Pole of the age. As we were con-
> versing there, Sheikh Abol-Hasan appeared looking ex-
> actly as I had left him in Kharaqan. I fainted and when I
> came to, it had been a full day and night. I begged those
> present to intercede for me and win the Sheikh's favor
> toward me. When He appeared again, He held my hand
> and when I came to, I was on Ray's[21] main thorough-
> fare. When I entered the Khaneqhah, my Sheikh said,
> "Son, what one sees in desolation, one does not speak
> of amidst crowds. I have begged my God to conceal me
> from everyone. Of creatures none has seen me except
> for Bayazid, and then, just a trifle."[22]

Stories and comments on Kharaqani could easily fill a separate book. What one may say in summary is that, in the vast
regions around his birthplace which have nurtured a very large

---

20 NbD, pp. 415-417.
21 An ancient city in northern Khorasan. It still exists today, though not as grand as it was
before the Mongol attack.
22 NbD, p. 243-244.

number of God-intoxicated lovers, he was, and is still, held in highest regard by those whose lives revolve around seeking nearness to that Presence from whom all existence emanates, has its life in and returns to. That Presence, which refuses to be named, and no matter what name we may apply to it, we only limit ourselves by forcing Infinity into a container of one form or another. Perhaps it would be best to conclude Sheikh Abol-Hasan Kharaqani's story with an anecdote that seems indicative of his approach.

It is said that one day the Sheikh and Amro, who was dear to him, were sitting under an immense tree in whose shade a multitude of sheep were resting. Amro said, "Sheikh, let us hold hands and jump on top of this tree!" Sheikh Kharaqani said, "Let us both hold God's hands and jump beyond both heaven and hell and pay attention to neither."[23]

---

23 NbD, p. 139, no. 6.

THE TEACHINGS

Our beloved Sheikh said,

How glorious this little human heart,
ailing in this Love and refusing to recover,
though everything in this creation
is offered at her feet.

And he said,

1 When I was rid of all that was below the Divine,
   I called my self, and I heard my Lord respond,
   and I knew I had left my animal qualities behind.
   I then honored the One who had summoned me,
   and obeyed, and becoming an Intimate, was allowed
        to enter
   and worship in the Oneness of Truth.
   Angels then sang my praises and I roamed pastures of
        Beauty.
   A Light appeared and within It, I beheld the abode
        of Truth,
   and by the time I reached It, of me was left Nothing.

2 I found my Beloved
   where I could not find myself.

3 In my heart I heard,
   "What I emptied you from, stay empty of,
   for I am that Living who never dies,
   and I'll give you that Life in which death has no place."

4   Beloved, take me to that Station
    where You Are,
    and I am not.

5   My Lord said, "I shall forgive creatures of earth
        and heavens
    but those who claim Nearness to me, I will not spare."
    And I said, be it as it may, regrets You shall find none
        here,
    let the dice fall where they may, for I shall withdraw
        nothing I have claimed."

6   The Beloved says, "I am the Road you travel,
    and I too am the Host that receives you;
    when you speak, I hear; when you think, I know;
    when you flee from me, I am your refuge;
    when you seek refuge, I am your shelter;
    your prayers I receive, and your hopes I fulfill;
    I am with you in desolation, and I am with you in
        your elation;
    be therefore Here, Now in This Presence."

7   Lord, I want to be with You,
     to appear in every creature as You,
     or to sink and disappear in You,
     without a trace.

8   Of Love a sign was given my heart,
     but I found no one in creation intimate enough
     to share It with.

9   Don't be meek in this Love,
     be kind to people, receive the wisdom of the Prophet's
         teachings,
     but don't be meek in this Love;
     for God is Bold and likes those who are bold in his
         Adoration...
     this Path is for the Bold, the Drunkard and the
         Lunatic;
     with God, Lunacy, Drunkenness, and Boldness works.

10 I do not tell you not to put in effort, but you need to
  remember who the Doer is;
you can trade only with God's capital, and when you
  offer it, in return,
you are taken in as one returning Home.
In the beginning you have Him only, and so it will be
  at the end,
and in the middle there's none else.
One who claims this place as his, won't find his way
  There.

11 One Bewildered in this Love,
is like unto a bird which leaves its nest in search of
  grain
and having found none,
cannot find its way back to its nest.

12 Traversing mountains in vain,
some develop calluses on their feet,
but those who are Admitted,
first have to develop calluses on their buttocks.*

*From sitting in meditation

13 Many interpret the Holy Book;
    Lovers interpret themselves.

14 Under this skin, there's an ocean,
    when Grace blows and this misty Intimacy awakens,
     it rains,
    and creation, from head to foot, is drenched in Love.

15 The Beloved said, "Abol-Hasan, do you
    want me to tell the world what I know of your
        wretchedness,
    and watch you be stoned to death?"
    and I said, "Do you want me to tell the world of your
        Infinite Tenderness and Mercy
    and watch the world stop praying to You?"
    and my Love said, "No more of this, neither from you,
        nor from me."

16 My Beloved said, "If you want me, be bold,
        for I am Bold,
    be pure, for I am Pure, and be needless,
    for I am Needless."

17 Archangel Gabriel appeared and
    I told him, I am from There and I know how to return
        There.
    And I asked my Beloved, "Why go-betweens,
    when your Presence never leaves my heart?"

18 When the devil cannot deceive you,
    then it is the Beloved who will offer you magic powers
    so as to keep you away,
    if not that, then He will bestow upon you his favors,
        withholding himself,
    but a Lover will not be deceived,
    for him the Beloved is the only Cure.

19 Be aware, He won't be wooed by prayer mats or robes,
whoever brings such airs will be crushed,
no matter what you dream yourself to be...
on the day of judgment, everyone is judged
    by their actions,
but those who claim Love, are judged by the Beloved,
and There, no slack is granted.
His claim on us is Final; our attachment to him, fierce.

20 The Beloved whispered this into my heart, "That self
which you seek, never had an existence to begin with;
this Journey is from God to God,
created beings cannot embark on this."

21 I begged my Beloved to take me to himself, and I heard,
"It is my command that whomever I love, shall come
    and see you,
and if not that, then hear your name, and fall in Love
    with you,
for I created you of my Purity, and none but the pure
    will fall in Love with you..."

22 All creation can fit in me,
but I can't find a trace of myself,
anywhere.

23 Choose Surrender, and your
journey home will be short.

24 One's heart is an ocean, and one's tongue is the shore;
one finds traces of what is in the ocean, on the shore.

25 I blossomed and brought forth my Self,
    like a branch brings forth flowers in the spring.

26 This Pain in the Lover's heart
    is not for the sky, for it'll collapse;
    It is not for the earth, for it'll sink;
    and It's not for the angels, for they'll lose forbearance
    and fall.

27 Lord,
    Abol-hasan won't brave your domain,
    for your Divine Guile is infinite.

28 Persist in modest piety and generosity
and keep the company of the True Lovers.

29 If one day you go out of your way by a thousand leagues
to avoid the power-hungry and the worldly,
you'll have gained a great deal that day.

30 The most meaningful occupation for
one's mind is the contemplation of the Friend.

31 I turned into dust,
    and an immense wind filled the seven skies with me,
    and I was nowhere to be found.

32 Under a thorn bush,
    with my Beloved in my heart, I'll be happy,
    under the tree of life, in the highest heaven,
    forgetful of my Love, I'll not live.

33 I taste, but I am not there;
    I hear, and I utter words,
    without being there.

34 I did not stop my penances
   till I held my hand out and a shimmering bar of gold
      appeared in it,
   I disregarded it, for whoever enters that gate,
   ends up being of the world, and does not fare well.

35 This, my life, is a moment in Worship.

36 I am quiet.
   To be in Presence and to speak
   is shameful.

37 I have been given That which the beginning, the end,
and time itself, is envious of.

38 I do not say that there's no hell or heaven,
but know that they are phenomenons,
and Here, where I reside with my Beloved,
there's no phenomenon.

39 I am that creature who has the seven skies,
and the seven earths, at his disposal.
Whatever I command to be, comes into being.
Where I am, there is no up, down, front, back, left or
right.

40 A moment there was
when every created being wailed and moaned for me
seeing my Pain.

41 My Beloved came to me amorously,
and when angels rose in jealousy,
He covered me from their sight,
and from all created beings' sights.

42 I revealed myself to creatures and all creatures
cried to the Lord,
and said, "we have seen no burden heavier than what
this one carries."
And my Beloved said, "... one who carries my Burden,
no one may behold
except in Gratitude, for they are Raised and Nourished
by me."

43 That which my Beloved gave me is like the sun,
    all else can be but stars,
    and all that was created has found its fruition in me...

44 I offered my heart, intellect, faith, and my self to
        my Beloved.
    I was then shown Purity, and It guided my deeds,
    till I reached a stage where all four of those became
        faithful servants.

45 What I know about my Lord
        is a great lot,
    what I do not know
        is greater yet;
    what I've divulged
        is that which could be understood.

46 I first imagined that I had been trusted with his
     Friendship,
  till it came to me that carrying the entire creation was
     an easier task,
  for I saw that it is his Godhood which He has
     entrusted us with.

47 Of my oneness with the One,
  I can speak to no one, for none would last.
  It'd be like holding a roaring flame to a bale of cotton.

48 Intellect cannot know its own origin.
  Many "wise" ones I have saved from the created.
  Where I am, intellect cannot reach.

49 Last night a Lover sighed;
    heaven and earth both burnt down.

50 My Beloved said, "I'll give you everything,"
    and I said, "Giving and taking is between strangers,
        no more of that."

51 Whoever considers himself a good man
        is not good;
    goodness is God's essence only.

52 I cannot be praised,
    whatever they say,
    in whatever language;
    I am not that.

53 Were it not for the Beloved's Command,
    I'd eat That which no created being can see,
    and live There where keepers of the Records
    can't find their way to.

54 I began in this place of uttering, hearing and knowing,
    but once I sank in the Ocean within,
    I was taken out of all such flea markets.

55 Bayazid said, "I am neither a traveler nor a resident."
     I say, "I am a traveler and a resident in my Beloved's
        Oneness."

56 Paths to God can't be counted,
     there are as many roads to him as there are humans.
     I was shown the path of Longing and told,
     "This is a heavy load, not everyone can bear it."

57 I begged for salvation and found it in solitude,
     I asked for safety and found it in silence.

58 For thirty years I have been speaking to my Lord only,
and people have thought it is them I am addressing.
I have uttered not a single insincere word,
for within and without I have only been with
my Beloved.
If the Prophet (Peace upon Him) were to walk through
this door now,
He would find the same and nothing else.

59 Like a snake which sheds its skin,
I've torn out of, and shed, my self.

60 There won't be a need for me
to stand ransom for those who come to me,
for they shall stand ransom for many.

61 Whoever heard or is hearing me,
the least that will be done for him
is that his trespasses shall not count.

62 I raised my face to my Lord and said,
My Beloved, on the day of reckoning,
judgment comes, and then all shall pass,
but that which is between You and me,
That, Never passes.

63 My Lord, your Joy is short-lived; mine, Eternal;
for You take delight in me,
but my Pleasure lies in You.

64 Anyone I hurt once turns away from me.
You I hurt daily, and yet, You are the One
always there for me.

65 When You call me
my soul comes alive,
when my heart remembers You,
my ego lets go of my Life.

66 Beloved, if my body fails and forsakes me, You heal me;
who would I run to if You forsook me?

67 Beloved, a heart of pure light, housed in a body of
     pure light,
   is still unworthy of You,
   what can one as impure as I am, hope for?

68 In every search, one always seeks and then journeys
     to find,
   except in this Affair
   where one is first Sought, and then only the journey
     begins.

69 Bayazid, the great Mystic, told his disciples,
   "God says whoever chooses me, I will do him
     great favors,
   whoever chooses Bayazid, I will annihilate him to be
     never remembered;
   now, who do you want?"
   "You," everyone declared.

70 A time will come when you will behold your heart
as a wave in the ocean,
a flame will appear from this wave, and burn
both your body and your heart to ashes,
the Tree of Fidelity will be nourished by these ashes,
and when you partake of the fruit of It,
your heart will be quenched, and you will disappear in
Oneness.

71 When one is filled with the Almighty,
from the hair on his head, to the bottom of his feet,
everything in him and on him gives witness to
the Presence
and his very breath proclaims Allah.

72 When It was Declared*, some heard "Aren't I God?";
some heard "Aren't I your Friend?", and some heard
"Aren't I your All?"

*Refers to a verse in the Qoraan.

73 The soul is like unto a bird,
   one of whose wings fills the west, the other, the east,
   its feet are in this lower creation,
   but its head is in a Place of which nothing can be said.

74 A little humility goes a lot further,
   than a lot of learning or austerity.

75 I looked at my seventy-three years of obedience,
   and it seemed as if an hour,
   I counted my years of rebellion, and my life stretched
      beyond Noah's years.

76 Only God is worthy of your mention,
   attention and adoration.

77 Philosophers speak of appearances, outer forms;
   Lovers sing to the world of Love.
   But the Inner Essence is between Lovers
       and their Truth,
   no one else can fit there.

78 Lovers have no interest in here or hereafter,
   for this world and the next are both too pale
       and profane,
   to compare with That which They treasure in
       their heart.

79 A true human is generous and kind to all creatures,
    and bringing all his needs to the Creator,
    stays needless of all else...

80 There are a thousand stations on this path,
    in the first one the ability to perform miracles
        is granted;
    those who accept it attain no other stations.

81 Whoever finds the Beloved
    does not remain,
    those who find the Beloved
    do not die!

82 A drop of Love from the Unseen came
and searched the hearts of all the lovers
and finding no one Intimate,
returned to the Unseen.

83 The heart that has anything in it other than the Almighty
is dead.

84 Nothing can stand between God and human except ego.
Everyone, even the Prophets, suffer because of it and
cry to their Lord.

85 The best conduct is to live in Remembrance,
   to be generous, to be sincere in piety,
   and to keep the company of those who abide in spirit.

86 Do not seek, till you are sought,
   for that which you are capable of finding,
   will, of essence, resemble you and be like you.

87 I was given a station where bestowers of
   miraculous powers gave me a wide berth;
   Khezr* stays aloof of me.

*Khezr (Farsi), Khidr (Arabic), The "Green Prophet," the Guide to the fountain of Life.

88 There are those whose heart is set aflame
with the Light of the Beloved's Presence,
so bright that if anything in creation passes near it,
it will burn like raw wool thrown into the fire.

89 Be Ambitious in this affair and set your sight on the
        highest,
and should He say, "I shall grant you Godhood,"
say you that giving and taking is for creatures;
        say Allah;
Allah beyond wanting; Allah beyond all; Allah beyond
        my soul; Allah!
Drunkenness is befitting one who has had Wine!

90 One who doesn't find God present in his speech
        and thoughts
will find trouble in both.

91 Everything can be scribed on, but water;
journey across this immense sea of life
and let your Longing scribe on it with your ashes the
story of your Love,
so those who will come behind you may know
that Torched, Drunken Lovers have passed through.

92 One may speak of those absent;
but one who is Ever Present,
one can say nothing of.

93 How can one who is Aflame at the bottom of an ocean,
be still?

94 The whole world seeks him,
   but only those He seeks,
   find him.

95 When you offer him your existence,
   He gives you his Life.

96 When one finds God in solitude,
   it is a sign that he loves God,
   but one who, in the midst of crowds,
   delights in the Beloved's Presence
   is Loved by God.

97　When He reveals you to yourself,
　　　you know all of creation,
　　　but when He reveals himself to you, That cannot be
　　　　described,
　　　for words can't find their way There.

98　One who takes no pity on creatures
　　　can't contain God's love in his heart.

99　One savors this Path in secrecy;
　　　revealed to others, it becomes ordinary.

100 Being content with what He wills is better
than a thousand self-willed acts of charity
which may not meet His approval!

101 A drop of Grace makes you desireless
of anything and any company.

102 Nothing is more arduous in this life
than harboring enmity with someone
for a day and a night.

103 You won't leave this realm till your eyes have bled in
     this Love,
     your entire being has melted in Awe,
     and your bones have thinned out in that Heat that
     keeps you awake.

104 Don't speak unless you know God is the Listener,
     do not listen unless you find him the Speaker.

105 One who is worthy of respect
     is blind, deaf and dumb to this world.

106 God distributed various things into his creation;
Lovers were granted Longing.

107 Lovers' heartache is beyond this world, and the next,
for they ever strive to praise their Beloved in a worthy
manner
and they never can.

108 Faith is when you see yourself with God.
when you see God in yourself, that is annihilation,
but when you see God and no one else,
you've found everlasting life.

109 One who thirsts after the Creator,
   is not quenched by anything created.

110 Man may call the Beloved and say Allah,
   or he may be absent from himself and utter Allah,
   or he may hear Allah in him call Allah.

111 This curtain between him and his creation is to protect it,
   for a few drops of Awareness would burn it all to
      ashes...

112 The Almighty spares none; his prophets are put to death
and his friends are whipped. He is Bold, truly Bold.
You be bold then and reach for nothing less than him.

113 There are many who walk the earth
and they are but dead;
and there are many whose bodies have long been
buried
and yet, they are Alive...

114 God's beloved are not seen except by those
who are granted this favor from Above;
and the more the disciple venerates the Master,
the more he is allowed to know about him.

115 You are to taste bitterness and sorrow here;
   once this is done, your life is with God.

116 I beheld his Glory, and my non-existence was revealed
      to me.
   I beheld my non-existence, his Glory was revealed
      to me...
   "This is beyond me," I moaned and came home with a
      black and blue heart
   and hid away in solitude.

117 For forty years now time has stood still
   and God looks into my heart and finds noone and
      nothing other than his own Presence.

118 Three things are difficult—
keeping God's Secrets,
controlling one's tongue,
and maintaining integrity.

119 Two types of evil-doers can cause more suffering than
the devil himself—
one who knows and exploits his knowing for worldly
gain,
and one who does not know, yet takes it upon himself
to preach to others.

120 One who sings a song through which he remembers
God worships;
one who reads the Holy Book but does not want God
does not.

121 Beloved if You grant me your friendship, I will drown in
    this Love.
    If you display your Sovereignty, I will be awed to
      insanity.
    But when this divine Boldness arises in me, I behold
      my Self in both, for You are my I-ness,
    You are the Abol-Hasanness in Abol-Hasan.

122 It is obvious who should abstain from what;
    yet the populace should abstain from sin,
    the preacher from preaching, the learned from
      knowledge,
    the ascetic from abstinence and the Lovers
    from asking the Lord for anything other than him.

123 The living have red blood,
    but the Lovers' blood is black and blue!

124 I told my heart, "Don't look in that Direction."
It would not obey and it burnt to ashes in the Fire of
Bliss,
and generously obliterated me as well.

125 In the hearts of the Lovers there are Pearls brought forth
by the Lord's Love
which never rise to their tongues,
though each is ten times the worth of the whole
world.

126 How beauteous to wander in the garden of the Beloved's
favors,
picking fruits from the tree of Faith, smelling the
flower of Adoration
and drinking the wine of Love, while of yourself you
are unable to find a trace.

127   There are 365 veins in your body and 365 bones
         and 365 joints, all of which at once praise their
            Creator
         in separate tongues, no one resembling the other.

128   The Beloved created this world
         and offered each group to choose their work and they
            did.
         One group remained standing, "... you, too," He said.
         "We have Lord," they said. "And what is that?"
         "We have chosen your Love," they said.
         Some are from this group; they have no other reason
            for being.

129   To taste this Love, be a fish in this Ocean.

130 Many things come from the heart of the mountains,
many from the oceans and deserts,
but compared to what is in the heart of a Lover,
all these are worth not a twig.

131 Everyone knows that one can't be with God
and be with himself, too.
Offer your Absence to receive this Presence,
offer your mortality to taste Eternity.

132 Sit at this Gate and cry, a year, two, ten,
twenty or thirty years. Finally, you'll be asked,
"What is it with you? What's ailing you?!"

133 Some asked for it and weren't given,
   some never asked and were given.

134 The Beloved whispered to my heart "My creature,
      be awake,
   whoever comes to visit your tomb, you will vouchsafe
      for them."
   Whoever does not believe that I'll be there when they
      stand in front of their Lord,
   let them not come near me.

135 The Lord said, "Declare your existence."
   I said, "Show my self to me, so I can declare it."
   The Beloved then said, "Declare my existence."
   And I said,
   "What is there that is not You? Haven't You ordered
      my soul to stand witness that other than You, isn't?" *

*Refers to a verse in the Qoraan.

136 My Lord made it known to me that whoever says two
   prayers in this abode,
   while I am here, or after I am gone, won't be shown to
   hell.

137 No matter who you are and what you have achieved,
   if you see yourself other than that naked, defenseless
      newborn in its mother's arms,
   you are like one who takes a gourd to the ocean and
      declares that he shall drink it all...

138 The Lord is pure of purity, the Prophet is pure by the
   Lord's purity
   and the Lover is pure by the Grace of the Lord and
      the Prophet.
   One who is not pure, deserves none of them.

139 Lovers are those who burden none
and their hearts, burning with the Love of the Lord,
warm up the hearts of others.

140 To walk in the Lord's company,
one has to have seen it all, heard it all, done it all,
and learned it all.

141 There are as many paths to the Lord
as there are grains of sand and drops of rain...
whoever seeks, eventually finds his way There.

142 To the wise, He said, "Mention my name as your belief
allows."
To the Lovers, He said," Mention my name the way I
deserve."

143 Abol-Hasan thought that Devotion meant bringing home
what the Beloved had left in trust in the human heart.
When I looked more closely,
I saw that the entire creation was trusted to the
Awakened human heart.

144 Those who reach the Truth
do so by the Grace of the Lord and his Word,
by the Message of his Messenger,
by obedience to the Master, and through that effort
which brings one to that Longing and Purity in
Action
in whose light one beholds the Beloved.
Then nothing but the Beloved remains.

145 Most of us try to take something There from here,
and there is nothing here that deserves to be There.
One who is true to one's Origin
struggles to bring That from There
which is so rare, and yet so sorely needed, here.

146 Three things I wanted to fathom and I never could,
the Lord's Glory, the Prophet's purity, and the depth
    of evil
in my ego.

147 One in whose heart the Lord's Purity lands,
becomes carefree of his own needs.

148 When one has done all that can be done,
one may hope to hear from the Lord, "Now I'll do the
   rest."
But if one has brought one's ignorance and desires,
then, one is told to pray, fast and make peace with
   one's enemies.

149 One who deserves to be praised is the Lord,
and one who deserves to be spoken of
and heard about is the Lord.

150 The Lord keeps everyone away through some device.
He gives himself to no one.

151 Everything smells of itself.
This world smells of non-existence.

152 If everything there is turns into gold
and is offered to you for a lie,
beware: do not fall.

153 There is a light that shines from the Lord onto humans,
and that is the light of Grace.
There is a light that seeks its way from humans to
the Lord,
and that is the light of Purity.

154 One who looks at humans with the Lord's eyes
forgives them.
One who looks at humans in true faith
finds them better than himself.

155 In heavens, Lovers smell the Beloved's Perfume,
evil doers smell the fire of hell,
and the faithful smell the breeze of paradise.

156 This Gate won't open except to true need and true
longing.

157 Love for your Lord you can't see in your heart,
until first you find compassion for his people,
and his creation, there.

158 Loving the Lord is like having a friend in a strange land,
when you travel there,
you'll find yourself less of a stranger.

159 Masters have said, "... one who obeys
does what the Beloved orders,
one who claims closeness
does that which the Beloved prefers,
but one who Loves
loves everything that befalls him."

160 When your heart reaches where it should,
you will hear your heart with your inner ear;
when the sound stops, light drowns everything
and you see the light of your heart with your inner
eyes.

161 It is said that someone took the Lord's name in front of
the Sheikh. Master said, "If He is with you, no
need to use this name, if He is not, the less you
gossip, the better."

162 Those who are with the Lord can't say anything,
those who speak of him
are not with him.

163 Abol-Hasan did not stop his penitence
        till he was assured by his Lord
        that he would be allowed to take anyone in this world
            he wanted,
        and walk him to heaven.

164 There are no words
        where Lovers reside
        but they come here to give the populace
            what they need,
        through their presence and utterance.

165 They asked the Sheikh what a disciple was and he said,
    "One who has no desires."

166 He was asked how one knows that the Lord is pleased
with him.
He said, "When one is pleased with the Lord and
loves everything the Lord does,
then the Lord is pleased with everything he does."

167 A Darveesh* is one in whose heart there's no worry,
one who utters words, but is not the speaker, one who
eats and drinks,
but his palate is not involved, one who is neither
mobile nor stationary.

168 We humans languish in this pain,
for we want to be Perfect and we can't,
and we long for the Perfect One.

---

*Darveesh (Farsi), one who has renounced "life" to walk the Path.

169 A disciple is one who in the first place respects
the Master,
the Lover of the Lord. And in the second place,
respects
the wishes of the Master, and in the third place,
adores him,
for He is that Lover who has no wishes,
and has given his very being to the Beloved.

170 Master was asked, "What is the cure for this pain?"
He said, "This Pain is its own Cure."

171 "Some do not understand Master's words," the Sheikh
was told.
He said, "This Light is seen by a certain light. This
is one of the Mysteries of the Lord...
to this Mystery not everyone is made an Intimate.
True Wisdom seeks a heart
with no worldly attachments and once found,
it alights there."

172 Master was asked if he was afraid of death. He said,
"Whatever everyone fears, of hells, the final judgment
and horrors of dying, is nothing compared to what
Abol-Hasan has gone through. And whatever
     heavens,
Beauty and Bliss everyone has been promised,
is nothing compared to what Abol-Hasan has within,
and looks forward to having."

173 Master was asked about repentance. He said, "Repent
from sin, repent from obedience and repent from
     faith!"

174 Masters manifest themselves in three ways:
in Mercy to the populace, in Truth,
and in that Reality where no words find their way.

175 "What is time?" he was asked. He said, "I do
not know. Time is the Lord's deeds.
Abol-Hasan can learn obedience,
but the Lord's deeds he cannot learn."

176 Whoever journeys on the road to the Lord faces three
pitfalls—
one is the desire for followers, another is hoarding
wealth,
and the last one is desire for name and fame.

177 A scattered heart will be declared by a scattered tongue.

178 All desires vanish from a heart that falls in Love with
the Lord.

179 Nothing pleases the Lord more than finding himself in
his Lover's heart
every time He looks there.

180 When I am with my Lord, I am in heaven,
when I am not with him, I'm in hell.

181 Do not go to your Lord carrying your penances
even if they conquered the seven skies,
do not go there feeling generous,
even if you have given away the whole world in
charity,
and do not go there carrying your sins, for you knew
when you committed them.
Go there empty and broken.

182 Do not injure your Lord's feelings, not for fear of
punishment,
but to avoid that sorrow that will assail you
when you realize in truth whose heart you have
broken.

183 No one who truly utters the Lord's name once can utter
it again,
for his tongue vanishes.

184 Keep your attention on the Lord
for He is the One to be Desired,
and He is the One to be Loved.

185 Neither life nor death should separate you from your
Beloved.

186 A Wayfarer is not one whose body is restless,
but one whose heart feels trapped in his body
and his Secret feels trapped in his heart.

187 Master was asked where anxiety came from.
He said, "Your heart is busied by three things:
that which you see, that which you hear,
and that which you put in your stomach.
When you look at, or listen to, that which
your mind should not contemplate, or when
your nourishment is gotten through unrighteous
means, you invite anxiety into your being."

188 In Mercy, the Lord chose a group to bear weapons and to
    ensure justice;
another to carry commerce in an equitable and just
    manner
and yet another to plant and harvest and provide
    wholesome nourishment.
He chose Lovers to behold him in their Solitude.

189 My Lord, most thank You for favors,
I thank You for Being.

190 My Lord said, "Those who bring their Need find me;
those who claim they have found me
are vying for crowd's attention and end in corruption."

191 My Lord told me, "Do with people that which I have
done with you."
I said I could not, and He said, "Ask for my help."

192 Abu-Yazid was asked if the individual's
struggle means anything on this path.
He said, "No, but neither can it be without."

193 When righteousness disappeared from among people, the Beloved hid his Friends.

194 Who am I to love You Lord,
I'll love those who Love You.

195 Unless the denizens of the eight regions descend to the first one,
they won't realize what they have missed.

196 I flee from You a thousand times a day
and every time You appear in a different garb and
ensnare me anew
and pay no heed to my screams and moans.
And when I am snared and begin pining for You, You
get mad at me
and ask me if I know my place and who and what I am
and if I know where You stand and where I stand.
Woe is me, woe is me.

197 I had been unable to cross beyond and was suffering this
obstacle,
I wondered if it would ever be conquered.
One night I saw myself standing in my Lord's
Presence,
Bayazid appeared and interceded for me,
my problem was solved immediately and darkness
lifted.
When he was leaving, Bayazid said smiling,
"O Abol-Hasan,
whoever asks God for nothing but God, his prayers
are answered."

198 Whoever knocks on this door
feed him and ask not of his faith
for if he deserved a Soul from his Creator,
he certainly deserves a loaf of bread from
Abol-Hasan.

199 How glorious this little human heart,
   ailing in this Love and refusing to recover
   though everything in this creation is offered
   at her feet.

200 Do not frighten me of hell
   or reward me with heaven,
   these two abodes are for others
   for me, there is only You!

201 My body is to work and replenish the earth,
   my tongue to speak of this Love,
   and my head to lay in surrender at my Beloved's feet.

202 My Lord had taken away my mind for many years
and presented me to the populace as a man
of wisdom.

203 The heart that has anything in it other than the
Almighty is dead.
When asked about his heart, Master said,
"I have been separated from my heart for forty years."

204 Should you meet a true Lover,
you may be sure that God has given you his blessing.

205 With God's creatures, I made peace,
and have not violated my vow.
To my ego I have delacred war,
and will never make peace.

206 For those who seek Him,
this creation is a trap
filled with obstacles
through one of which
He may wish to reach us.

207 If your heart is with the Beloved
and the whole world hangs around your neck,
no loss.
If your heart is not with the Beloved,
whether you go around in rags, or in gold stitched silk,
no gain.

208 Those who, by the crowds' measure, are childlike,
are Men in God's sight;
those upheld as men here
are deemed but childish There.

209 God reveals only his creation to us,
for if He revealed himself,
no one would last long enough to declare,
*"la ilaha illallah."**

210 Whatever is in seven skies and in seven regions
is all inside you,
you just need to see it.

*Arabic: "There is no god but God."

211 Whoever burns down in this Longing,
the breeze of Love blows his Ashes around
and the sky is filled with It...

212 One who falls in Love with God, finds him;
one who finds him, loses himself!

213 Tomorrow when they ask me,
"What were you doing and what have you brought?"
I'll say, "This dog of an ego,
which I spent a lifetime watching,
so it wouldn't fall upon me or others,
and this mind full of filth,
which I spent my life trying to purify.

214 It is said that Master beheld the Almighty in a dream one
night
and said, "My Lord, for sixty years I have lived Pining
for You,"
and he was told, "So you have, for sixty years, but
I chose you on the day before the first day;
that is when this Friendship was declared,
who then was first to Love?"

215 Master said, "I begged my Creator to let me see myself as
I am,
and behold, I saw an old, threadbare garment,
unworthy of a glance,
and I asked, 'Is this me?' "
and I was reassured, "Yes, indeed!"
and I begged, "All of our moaning, devotion, longing
and tears...what are those?"
and my Beloved said, "I
Am all that."

216 Anyone who goes through a day without hurting anyone
may consider that day to have been spent in the
Prophet's company.

217 An old man was asked how he was,
and he said, "How can one feel from whom God
demands purity,
while the devil lurks in his mind, watching,
the Prophet demands obedience,
the angel of death demands his life,
his desires demand fulfillment,
his family demands sustenance,
and the king's tax collector is knocking on his door?"

218 One day I raised my head and said,
"How strange that this Longing for You never leaves
my heart."
I heard, "It is that Longing that keeps you alive!"

219 What we need,
the Lord is pleased to grant us daily.
Come Lovers, let us offer our hearts at his feet daily.

220 Taking a single breath with God is better than
whatever all earths and heavens may dream of.

221 Fasts and prayers are good,
yet, purifying your heart from arrogance, jealousy
and greed is better,
for your heart is where God acknowledges you.

222 The Beloved keeps everyone away
by busying them with trinkets;
He gives himself to no one.
O' Lovers, be steadfast and Awake
so you are not sent away after a trifle.

223 If one should ask you
how a mortal may see the Eternal,
say that today, in this temporal abode,
a mortal develops that Thirst
which tomorrow will illuminate his way There.

224 The Lover faces God in Adoration,
and the seeker adores his face;
the Lover becomes a messenger,
for the seeker to behold the Message,
the Lover is God's charge,
the seeker, the Lover's.

225 One who does not taste the Delight and Delicacy of
     God's Word,
     before he dies,
     has received nothing from this life.

226 Master was asked of the Great Name...
     He said, "It is that Name in which The One remains,
     and all otherness dissolves"...

227 We do not come to the Beloved,
   He pulls us to himself,
   and though needless of all,
   spreads his generous table of Grace and Mercy
   and declares, "My Beggars, it is for the Secret Sacrament
   between us that you are summoned."*

228 If He didn't remember us,
   we could not be reminded of him.
   We give Thanks because one like him,
   remembers the likes of us.

229 Mohammad ibn-ol Hosein, who had great devotion to
   our Sheikh, said that once he was sick and
   frightened of death, Master told him not to be
   afraid and promised to be present at his death bed,
   "...should it come thirty years after my death."
When he was dying, his son saw him stand up in his
   last moment and loudly implore, "Enter, and may
   Peace be upon You, too." And he said, "...son,
   Sheikh Abol-Hasan has kept his word after all
   these years and has come, so I won't be afraid."
Then he breathed his last.

---

* *Tafseer-e Adabi va Erfani Qoraan-e Majid* (Abridged Farsi version) / *Literary and Mystical Interpretations of the Quraan.* Vol. II, Adapted from the ten volume *Khashf-ol-asrar* by Khaje Abdollah Ansari (Original Arabic), Imam Mohammad Meybodee and Habeeb-ollah Amoozgar, editors. Tehran, Iran: Eqbal Publications, original ©1993, new edition 2004, page 24.

230 When Master's time had come, he said, "I wish my heart,
bloodied in this Affair, could be displayed so
everyone could see that with God, idol worship
does not bode well."
Then he demanded to be buried thirty feet deep so as
his tomb may not be above that of Bayazid's
in nearby Bastam. "It'd be ill manners," he said.
The day after his burial a great snow storm covered
the land and a huge stone was found atop Master's
tomb and there were lions' footprints all around it.

231 Master was seen in a dream and was asked, "What did
the Almighty say to you?"
He said, "He handed me the register of my deeds and
I said, "You knew well what I was capable of before
my actual deeds and I well know what I am, let
those who wrote this, read it and let me be with
You for a spell and breathe with your chest."

APPENDIX

In Praise of Sheikh Abol-Hasan Kharaqani
Mehdi Akhavan Saales (d. 1990)

You of Pure Birth, whose Kharaqan the holy dome of Kaaba
    adores,
Son of dust risen to the highest abode, purer than pure,
    Abol Hasan of Kharaqan,
thornless roses so beauteous and fragrant, have risen but few
    on this dusty plane,

blazing to the highest heaven, becoming our tongue of flame,
none has been as Bold as you in this fierce game,
released from intellect's croak, from Love itself you received
    your cloak,
Prince of the region of Love beyond regions of blame,

with a heart parched with longing, you sing to us the joys of
    true victory,
and raise the station of the human higher than high,
O' Son of dust become worthy of True Glory,

I have called you many things, and more, yet I have failed you
    and withheld sorely,
for when it comes to you, the hope to praise is itself a folly,
Son of dust become purer than pure, precious else can be said
    of this story.[1]

---

1 *In Praise of Sheikh Abol-Hasan Kharaqani* by Mehdi Akhavan Saales, (NbD, pp. 19-21).
Rendition by Vraje Abramian.

REFERENCES

Unless otherwise specified, page numbers refer to: Kadkani, Dr. Mohammad Reza Shafiee. *Neveshte-bar-darya, az miras-e erfani-e Sheikh Abol-Hasan-e Kharaqani* (Original Farsi) / *Scripture on the Sea, from Spiritual Legacy of Sheikh Abol-Hasan of Kharaqan*. Tehran, Iran: Sokhan Publications, 1988.

#	Reference	#	Reference
1	p.164, no. 100	21	p. 163, no. 94
2	p. 46, no. 316	22	p. 48, no. 4
3	p. 172, no. 184	23	p. 49, no. 17
4	p. 181, no. 197	24	p. 50, no. 21
5	p. 180, no. 187	25	p. 50, no. 17
6	p. 290, no. 757	26	p. 56, no. 9
7	p. 181, no. 199	27	p. 59, no. 703
8	p. 176, no. 170	28	p. 72
9	p. 211, nos. 395 & 396	29	p. 72
10	p. 200, no. 319	30	p. 72
11	p. 209, no. 378	31	p. 154, no. 43
12	p. 184, no. 217	32	p. 156, no. 56
13	p. 48, no. 8	33	p. 157, no. 60
14	p.49, no. 10	34	p. 157, no. 61
15	p. 45	35	p. 160, no. 81
16	p.47, no. 395	36	p. 159, no. 75
17	p. 45, no. 2	37	p. 160, no. 78
18	p. 216, no. 428	38	p. 160, no. 78
19	p. 201, no. 321	39	p. 160, no. 79
20	p. 190, no. 250	40	p. 161, no. 83

#	Reference	#	Reference
41	p. 161, no. 85	69	p. 184, no. 218
42	p. 163, no. 95	70	p. 186, no. 225
43	p. 163, no. 97	71	p. 187, no. 230
44	p. 163, no. 96	72	p. 187, no. 232
45	p. 163, no. 98	73	p. 188, no. 235
46	p. 165, no. 104	74	p. 188, no. 239
47	p. 156, no. 108	75	p. 190, no. 252
48	p. 166, no. 112	76	p. 191, no. 257
49	p. 168, no. 125	77	p. 194, no. 277
50	p. 59	78	p. 194, no. 279
51	p. 169, no. 130	79	p. 195, no. 281
52	p. 167, no. 118	80	p. 197, no. 295
53	p. 169, no. 139	81	p. 197, no. 297
54	p. 170, no. 135	82	p. 197, no. 298
55	p. 174, no. 156	83	p. 198, no. 301
56	p. 171, no. 140	84	p. 198, no. 304
57	p. 172, no. 142	85	p. 198, no. 308
58	p. 175, no. 164	86	p. 199, no. 312
59	p. 174, no. 155	87	p. 182, no. 207
60	p. 177, no. 175	88	p. 186, no. 226
61	p. 178, no. 176	89	p. 201, no. 322
62	p. 180, no. 188	90	p. 201, no. 325
63	p. 180, no. 190	91	p. 202, no. 333
64	p. 198, no. 181	92	p. 202, no. 342
65	p. 182, no. 207	93	p. 204, no. 346
66	p. 183, no. 208	94	p. 205, no. 348
67	p. 183, no. 211	95	p. 206, no. 358
68	p. 184	96	p. 206, no. 306

#	Reference
97	p. 206, no. 362
98	p. 207, no. 365
99	p. 209, no. 381
100	p. 210, no. 384
101	p. 210, no. 385
102	p. 386, no. 210
103	p. 211, no. 398
104	p. 212, no. 401
105	p. 209, no. 376
106	p. 209, no. 380
107	p. 212, no. 403
108	p. 212, no. 405
109	p. 213, no. 411
110	p. 214, no. 412
111	p. 214, no. 415
112	p. 214, no. 416
113	p. 215, no. 418
114	p. 217, no. 434
115	p. 218, no. 441
116	p. 230, no. 504
117	p. 244, no. 510
118	p. 250, no. 555
119	p. 251, no. 556
120	p. 263, no. 622
121	p. 281, no. 698
122	p. 284, no. 720
123	p. 285, no. 722
124	p. 287, no. 736

#	Reference
125	p. 287, no. 737
126	p. 287, no. 737
127	p. 287, no. 743
128	p. 288, no. 745
129	p. 287, no. 741
130	p. 287, no. 742
131	p. 289, no. 749
132	p. 289, no. 753
133	p. 290, no. 754
134	p. 290, no. 758
135	p. 291, no. 760
136	p. 292, no. 764
137	p. 294, no. 775
138	p. 295, no. 779
139	p. 295, no. 780
140	p. 296, no. 785
141	p. 296, no. 784
142	p. 297, no. 787
143	p. 297, no. 786
144	p. 297, no. 788
145	p. 297, no. 789
146	p. 300, no. 803
147	p. 303, no. 824
148	p. 306, no. 837
149	p. 306, no. 840
150	p. 307, no. 846
151	p. 307, no. 848
152	p. 307, no. 850

#	Reference
153	p. 309, no. 860
154	p. 310, no. 865
155	p. 310, no. 869
156	p. 312, no. 883
157	p. 313, no. 887
158	p. 313, no. 888
159	p. 313, no. 893
160	p. 314, no. 898
161	p. 316, no. 906
162	p. 316, no. 908
163	p. 319, no. 930
164	p. 320, no. 935
165	p. 322, no. 944
166	p. 328, no. 946
167	p. 323, no. 948
168	p. 324, no. 956
169	p. 325, no. 959
170	p. 330, no. 989
171	p. 326, no. 964
172	p. 327, no. 968
173	p. 329, no. 979
174	p. 329, no. 982
175	p. 330, no. 983
176	p. 330, no. 985
177	p. 330, no. 990
178	p. 331, no. 994
179	p. 331, no. 995
180	p. 332, no. 1005

#	Reference
181	p. 333, no. 1011
182	p. 334, no. 1014
183	p. 333, no. 1009
184	p. 335, no. 1018
185	p. 695, Neyshaboori, Sheikh Farideddin Attar. *Tazkarat-ol-Olya* (Original Farsi) / *Biographies of the Saints.* Dr. Mohammad Estelamee, editor.Tehran, Iran: Zavvar Publications, 1994.
186	p. 338, no. 1122
187	p. 339, no. 1026
188	p. 344, no. 1050
189	p. 346, no. 1063
190	p. 348, no. 1075
191	p. 348, no. 1067
192	p. 357, no. 1108
193	p. 388, no. 1189
194	p. 388, no. 1190
195	p. 393, no. 1213
196	p. 395, no. 1222
197	p. 424, no. 1298
198	p. 76
199	p. 287, no. 738
200	p. 214, no. 413
201	p. 74, no. 5
202	p. 170, no. 133
203	p. 198, no. 301

#	Reference		#	Reference
204	p. 199, no. 309		224	p. 288, no. 710
205	p. 173, no. 152		225	p. 211, no. 394
206	p. 208, no. 368		226	p. 221, no. 462
207	p. 212, no. 404		227	*Tafseer-e Adabi va Erfani Qoraan-e Majid* (Abridged Farsi version) / *Literary and Mystical Interpretations of the Quraan*. Volumes I and II. Adapted from the ten volume *Khashf-ol-asrar* by Khaje Abdollah Ansari (Original Arabic), Imam Mohammad Meybodee and Habeeb-ollah Amoozgar, editors. Tehran, Iran: Eqbal Publications, third edition 2004, c1993., vol. 2, p. 24.
208	p. 213, no. 406			
209	p. 213, no. 408			
210	p. 215, no. 421			
211	p. 215, no. 422			
212	p. 220, no. 451			
213	p. 228, no. 495			
214	p. 229, no. 500			
215	p. 230, no. 503			
216	p. 251, no. 562			
217	p. 256, no. 588			
218	p. 281, no. 697			
219	p. 297, no. 790		228	p. 309, no. 864
220	p. 14, no. 96		229	p. 231, no. 507
221	p. 210, no. 387		230	p. 230, no. 505
222	p. 214, no. 417		231	p. 231, no. 506
223	p. 217, no. 433		Appendix pp. 19 - 21	

BIBLIOGRAPHY

Abramian, Vraje, translator. *This Heavenly Wine: Poems from the* Divan-e Jami. Renditions by Vraje Abramian. Prescott, Arizona: Hohm Press, 2006.

Danner, V., Thackson, W.M., and Annemarie Shimmel. "Ibn Ata' Illah. The Book of Wisdom, Kwaja Abdullah Ansari, Intimate Conversations." In: *The Classics of Western Spirituality*. New York: Paulist Press, 1978.

Kadkani, Dr. Mohammad Reza Shafiee. *Neveshte-bar-darya, az miras-e erfani-e Sheikh Abol-Hasan-e Kharaqani* (Original Farsi): *Scripture on the Sea, from Spiritual Legacy of Sheikh Abol-Hasan of Kharaqan*. Tehran, Iran: Sokhan Publications,1988.

Lao Tsu. *Tao Te Ching: A New Translation* by Gia-fu Feng and Jane English. New York: Vintage Books, a division of Random House, 1927.

Shams Tabrizi. *Maqhalate Sham-e Tabrizi" Bazkhani-e Motoon / Essays of Shams Tabrizi*. Jafar Modares Sadeqhi, editor. Tehran, Iran: Markaz Publications, 1977.

Neyshaboori, Sheikh Farideddin Attar. *Tazkarat-ol-Olya* (Original Farsi) / *Biographies of the Saints*. Dr. Mohammad Estelamee, editor.Tehran, Iran: Zavvar Publications, 1994.

Tafseer-e Adabi va Erfani Qoraan-e Majid (Abridged Farsi version) / *Literary and Mystical Interpretations of the Quraan*. Volumes I and II. Adapted from the ten volume *Khashf-ol-asrar* by Khaje Abdollah Ansari (Original Arabic), Imam Mohammad Meybodee and Habeeb-ollah Amoozgar, editors. Tehran, Iran: Eqbal Publications, original © 1993, new edition 2004.